Gratitude bestows reverence, allowing us to encounter everyday epiphanies, those transcendent moments of awe that change forever how we experience life and the world. John Milton

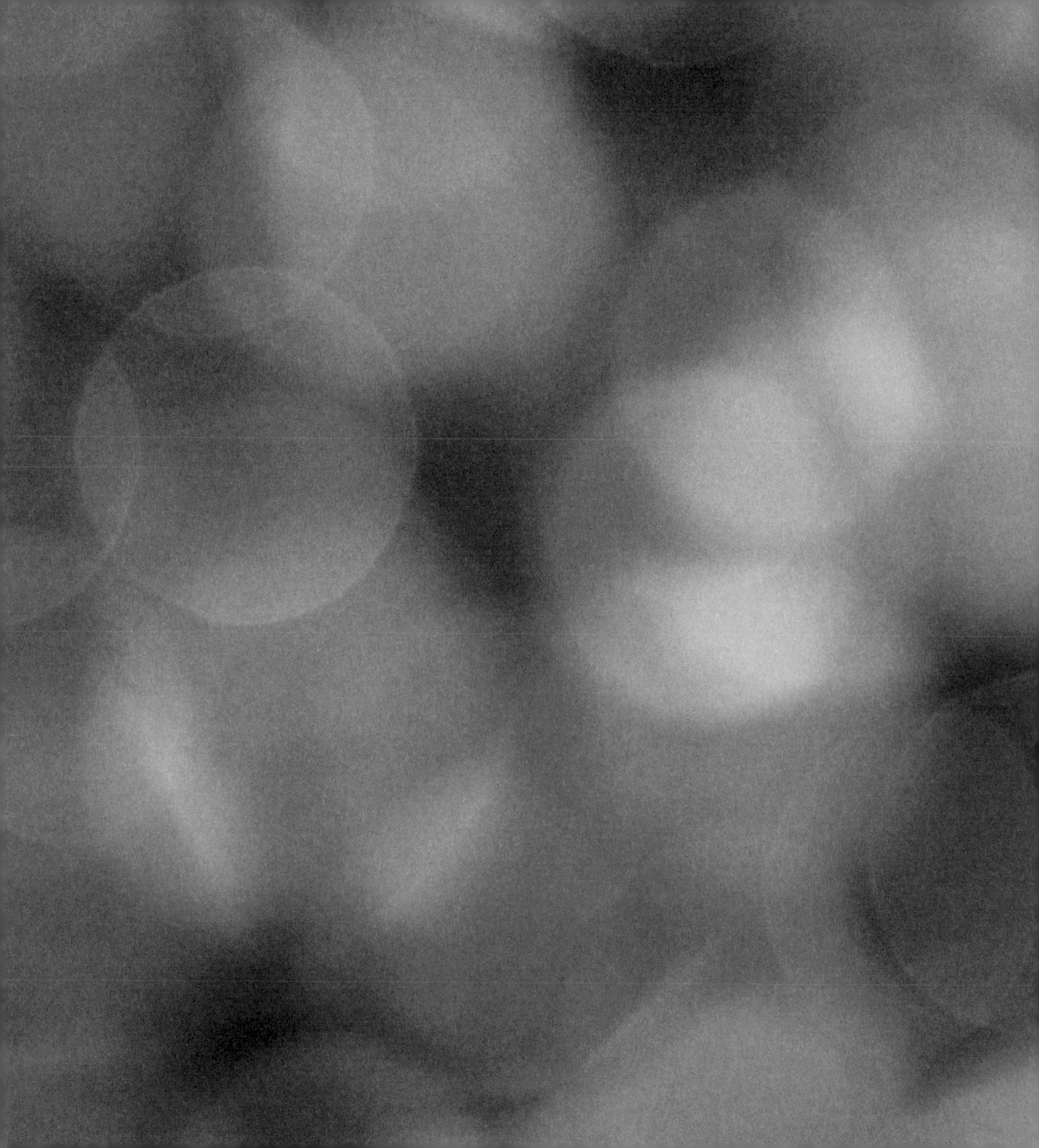

The Note

by Mike O'Mary

Published by Dream of Things
Chicago, IL
dreamofthings.com

For more information regarding special
discounts for bulk purchases, please write
to customerservice@dreamofthings.com.

ISBN 978-0-9825794-0-4

Design: McMillan Media

Photography: Kathy Hayevsky, "Man Leaving"
(page 10) and "The Note" (page 34). "Orphanage" (page 12) courtesy of Philip Howard,
theirhistory.co.uk. O'Mary family photos.

Acknowledgements: Thank you for permission
to reprint quotes to Dr. Wayne Dyer, *The Power
of Intention*, copyright©2004, Hay House,
Carlsbad, CA, and Joanna L. Krotz, Muse2Muse
Productions, a New York custom content
provider, and contributor to the Microsoft Sma
Business Center.

Dedicated, with love, to Sharon O'Mary Cheste
author of the original note.

Special thanks to Kathy and Kathleen for their
support and encouragement, and to Michael
for all his help on *The Note*.

Printed in Mexico.

TABLE OF CONTENTS

INTRODUCTION

How can a "thank you" note have a profound, life-changing effect on someone? Simple. When it comes from one heart and connects to another.

When I first read *The Note*, I was struck by the underlying sadness – and it's true: the story behind the note will break your heart. But by the time you finish reading, your heart will be mended and filled with warmth. The powerful and ultimately uplifting message is that a simple note can change the life of another person.

I have known Mike O'Mary for 21 years, and have always admired his ability as a writer. Mike has a gift for simple, frank exposition of life's most poignant moments, and in *The Note*, he shares that gift with all of us. Mike also provides insight into the importance of showing appreciation and sharing our feelings. His step-by-step advice on "Writing a Heartfelt Note" provides inspiration while removing the roadblocks that often prevent us from sharing important thoughts and memories with those who have touched our lives. A simple note of appreciation has an impact far beyond the words themselves. It can rekindle memories and emotions from across an entire lifetime, and create positive feelings that ripple outwards and touch an ever-expanding circle of people, including friends, family, neighbors, coworkers – and all who read this book.

How many times do you wish you had said "thank you" or shared a thought or memory with someone when you had the chance? We can't go back in time, but we don't have to let another opportunity pass. Read this book and take action. Your actions can change someone's life – and by extension, create a better world.

Michael McMillan

The Note

by Mike O'Mary

One Christmas, I received a note from my sister.

The note made me very happy,

but it also made me cry.

thought

of you

It was very personal, so I kept it to myself for a long time.

But it has had such a profound and lasting effect on me

that I decided to share it with others.

I'll show you the note, but first, I have to tell you a few things

about my sister and our family.

Our parents got divorced when I was ten.

My youngest sister, Sharon, was two.

Sharon and I, along with the rest of our brothers

and sisters, stayed with our mother.

Our father remarried and moved away.

Mom tried her best, but it was hard to make ends meet.

So a few years later...

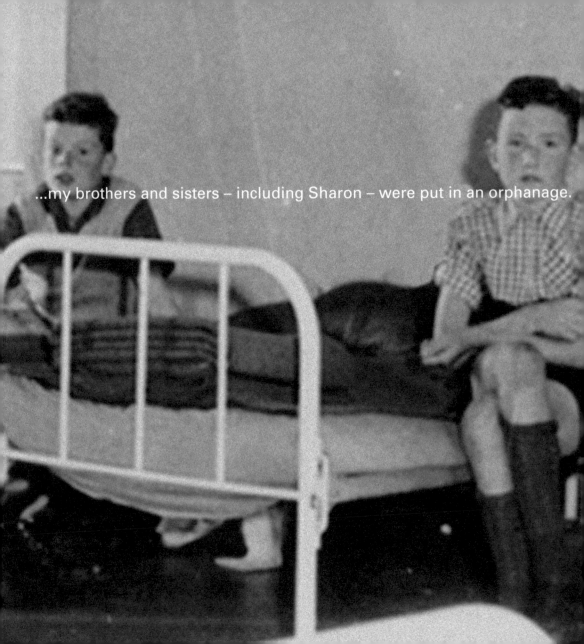

...my brothers and sisters – including Sharon – were put in an orphanage.

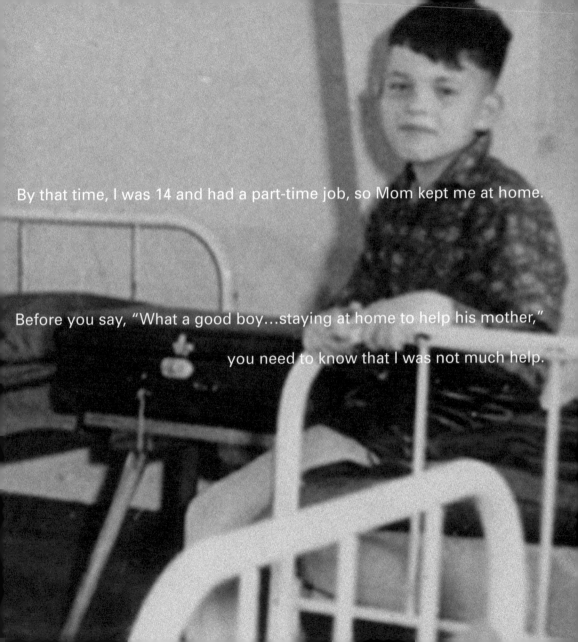

By that time, I was 14 and had a part-time job, so Mom kept me at home.

Before you say, "What a good boy...staying at home to help his mother," you need to know that I was not much help.

In fact, I was nothing but trouble.

I skipped school…stayed out late at night…

even got arrested

and put on probation for shoplifting.

The culminating event came when I skipped school one day, stole Mom's car...

...and wrecked it.

After that, I went to live with my father.

And as a result, I never had a chance to get to know Sharon.

That bothered me a lot as I grew up

and began to realize how important family is.

I went home to visit each year, and I tried to make each visit special.

But I could never make up for the past.

My brothers and sisters are all grown now.

Sharon is married and has her own life: husband, daughter,

son, career, the works.

A lot of years have gone by.

And all those years, I never knew what, if anything,

she thought of me and my visits.

Then I received this note from my little sister one Christmas:

Dear Mike,

I have a special memory of one of the times you came home to visit...

It was Christmas Eve and we didn't have a tree yet...

so you took me out to get one.

FRESH *Chris*...

It was the first time I ever got to pick out a tree

Now every year when we're going to get a Christmas tree,

I think of you and that visit...

...and I smile.

a special men—

of the time y—

home to visit. I

Sue and w—

a few yet

out to

the

to

Now every year when I'm
going to get a Christmas
tree, I think of you +
visit, and I smile.
Thanks.
Love,
Sharon

That's the note, and I'm sharing it

because if there's anybody special out there...

a brother, sister, father or mother...

a neighbor, friend, teacher or coworker...

and if there is any reason to suspect

they don't know how you feel...

...for God's sake, tell them.

I guarantee they'll appreciate it.

Every note you send

matters more than

you can imagine.

Every person you embrace makes the world a better place.

Open your heart today

and tell someone

how you feel.

WRITING A HEARTFELT NOTE

I sincerely believe one of the most beautiful and powerful things any of us can do is to let other people in our lives know they are appreciated.

When I first received the note from my sister, I was deeply touched. More than 20 years had passed since I took her to get that Christmas tree. And to tell the truth, I hadn't realized the significance of that event to her.

After I received Sharon's note, I thanked her for it and told her how much it meant to me. I also sat down and wrote a few thank you notes of my own that were long overdue. Then I put the note away and went back to business as usual. Except I couldn't get the note out of my mind. I found myself going back to it and rereading it often. Sharon's simple words of appreciation healed years of doubt. I now know that my visits back home made a difference.

Then one day while rereading Sharon's note, I realized I should share it with others. So I wrote an essay about Sharon and the note that was published in the *Peoria Journal-Star,* and readers contacted me to tell me how much the story meant to them.

After that, I told the story to more people. And each time, I could see the impact it had on them. That's why I'm sharing it with you. My hope is that the story will inspire and motivate you to share your appreciation of people in your life. I can tell you firsthand that a simple note can change the recipient's life. Equally important, showing appreciation and sharing your positive feelings with others can change *your* life.

I said at the outset that letting someone know they are appreciated is one of the most beautiful and powerful things one human being can do for another. Think about it: what would make you feel good about yourself and your time here on Earth? Wouldn't it feel good to receive a note thanking you for something nice that you did, telling you that you are appreciated, or letting you know that you made a difference?

Imagine receiving a note from an old friend, a neighbor or a relative you haven't talked to in a long time. Or, perhaps even more special, imagine getting a note from someone you see almost every day...your son, daughter, spouse, best friend or coworker. Wouldn't that make you feel great? Of course it would!

The Golden Rule says, "Do unto others as you would have them do unto you." You just envisioned how good it would feel to "have them do unto you." Now imagine the good feelings you can create among your family and friends when you share your appreciation with them. You can be sure that when you "do unto others" and share your positive feelings about them, you are going to make them feel good, too.

And here's a bonus for you: it also feels great to send someone a note! You will feel so good after telling people how you feel, you won't believe it. You will feel good because you set those emotions free instead of holding them in, and because by thanking someone for doing good, you will have done good. It's a great feeling.

There are other benefits to sharing your positive feelings with others. I consider a note of appreciation to be an act of kindness, and noted author and motivational speaker Dr. Wayne Dyer talks in his book, *The Power of Intention*, about the multiple benefits of acts of kindness: "Research has shown that a simple act of kindness directed toward another human being improves the functioning of the immune system and stimulates the production of serotonin in both the recipient of the kindness and the person extending the kindness. Even more amazing is that persons observing the act of kindness have similar beneficial results.

Kindness extended, received or observed beneficially impacts the physical health and feelings of everyone involved."

Now here's the really exciting news: YOU have the power to get the ball rolling and make these good feelings happen! You can share your feelings with the people you appreciate and care about, and as a result, many of them will be inspired to do the same.

The heart has an infinite capacity for love. You just have to open up and let it out. It's that simple. The love you create by sharing your appreciation of others will grow exponentially as it passes from you to your friends and relatives, and from them to their friends and relatives, and so on, like ever-expanding ripples across the global pond.

SO... WHAT'S STOPPING YOU?

WHY PEOPLE DON'T WRITE THANK YOU NOTES

In the next section, I will share with you some fun steps you can follow to help you get started with writing a heartfelt note of appreciation. But first, I want to acknowledge some common reasons (also known as "excuses") people cite for not sharing their feelings or letting others know they are appreciated. I have also included some thoughts on why you should ignore these reasons/excuses.

There is more hunger for love and appreciation in this world than for bread. Mother Teresa

Excuse #1: "I don't have time."

We all have multiple commitments...work, family, bills, home improvement projects, household chores...the list goes on and on. Often, we intend to say "thank you," but never seem to find the time. Then the "thank you" falls into the category of "unfinished business" – and nobody feels good about unfinished business.

But when it comes to return on investment, saying "thank you" is one of the most rewarding investments you can make. As Dr. Dyer noted, there are benefits to the physical and emotional health of everyone involved. And it really does not take much time to send a note to someone. Look at how short the note from my sister was. You only need to write a few words, and in the next section, "Four Fun Steps to Letting Someone Know How You Feel," I will show you how easy it is.

Excuse #2: "I don't know where to begin," or "I don't know what to say."

There is something about putting ink on paper that can be intimidating.

Even top executives at some of the largest companies in the world are

intimidated when it comes to writing – I know because I have made my

living over the past 20 years by writing for them! I am going to help you,

too. The steps in the next section will help you get started. Again, you

only need to write a few words. And if writing even just a few words is

intimidating, you can use a thank you card to help express your feelings.

You will find unique and beautiful cards and e-cards at dreamofthings.com.

Gratitude is a quality similar to electricity: it must be produced and

discharged and used up in order to exist at all. William Faulkner

Excuse #3: "They already know how I feel."

Are you sure? How do they know? Are they mind readers? Did a little

birdie tell them? Chances are, they don't know. And even if you said

something nice about them to somebody else and they eventually heard

about it indirectly, that's not the same as hearing it directly from you.

How many times have you heard, "Hey, so-and-so said you did a great

job"? Don't you wish so-and-so had said those things directly to you?

The only way to be sure someone knows how you feel is to tell the

person yourself – and there's nobody they'd rather hear it from than *you.*

Excuse #4: "Nobody ever says 'thank you' to me."

When people use "nobody ever tells me" as an excuse, my first response

is to ask them, "Is that really true?" Chances are it's probably not true.

They are just feeling a little down or even feeling sorry for themselves.

But if it is true, maybe they need to do more good – and one way to

do good is to get the ball rolling by letting others know you appreciate

them. It's a little like parties: sometimes you don't get invited to them

unless you throw a few yourself.

The deepest principle in human nature is the craving to

be appreciated. William James

Excuse #5: "Writing a thank you note is old-fashioned."

When I hear this excuse, I wonder which part is considered "old-fashioned" – the idea of writing a note (versus typing, e-mailing or texting), or the whole idea of saying "thank you." If you think writing a note is old-fashioned, then by all means use whatever communication channel you like. The important thing is to let the other person know how you feel. And to people who think the whole idea of saying "thank you" is old-fashioned, I say, "Hogwash!" Granted, there was a time (before the Internet, e-mail, cell phones and cheap long-distance rates) when writing thank you notes (and writing letters in general) was more the norm. But the fact that people have less time to write thank you notes doesn't make such notes old-fashioned; it just makes them more rare – and therefore even more valuable and appreciated.

4

FOUR FUN STEPS TO LETTING SOMEONE KNOW HOW YOU FEEL

Some people don't need any help when it comes to writing notes and sharing their feelings. They know who they want (or need) to write to, and they know exactly what they want to say. If you are one of those people, maybe reading *The Note* was all you needed to inspire you, and now you are ready to pick up pen and paper and start writing. If so, please feel free to skip ahead to Step #4 of this section – or to skip this section altogether and go write a note.

But if you are like me, you might need a little help to get started. That's okay...it's easy...and it's fun! You will still need to pick up a pen and paper, but that's about as hard as it's going to get. Let's get started.

Nothing is more honorable than a grateful heart. Seneca

STEP #1: WRITE DOWN TWO OR THREE NAMES

Start by making a short list of names. It can be really short: you only need two or three names to start. Think of friends, family members, neighbors and coworkers. You might also want to think back to other times in your life...to elementary school, high school or college...to past employers, places where you used to live, organizations you belonged to, etc. Perhaps you will think of a teacher, a mentor, an old friend, your first boss or a former coworker. Think particularly about people you like or admire.

When I did Step One, I thought of my parents, my siblings and my daughter. I also thought of my aunts, uncles, cousins and other relatives. My Great Aunt Nina, for example, let us spend our summer vacations with her when I was a little kid. She lived on an orange grove outside of Tampa in the 1960s. It was a great place to visit, and it was the only way our family could afford a Florida vacation.

I also thought of Mary Litoni, our next door neighbor when I was a child; Gurdon, a long-time friend from my college days who I only see once or twice a year now; and June, one of my first customers when I began working as a consultant.

Again, you only need two or three names to get started. If you want to list more, that's fine. As soon as you have a few names and are ready to move on, go to Step Two.

TIP: As you make your list, you may think of some people who are no longer with us. That's okay. You don't want to discard those names or your memories of those people. Those names go on a special list, and I'll give you some suggestions for what to do with them in the section titled "Special Events and Circumstances."

STEP #2: DESCRIBE THEM

Now pick one person from your list and describe that person. When I say "describe" them, I am not talking about a physical description – although you are free to do that too if it helps. No, I want you to describe the personality, key traits and strengths of the person. If somebody asked you to describe this person in one or two words, what would you say? Is he smart...funny...witty...charming? Is she helpful...optimistic... upbeat...energetic? What other words can you think of to describe the people on your list? Again, you only need to come up with two or three words to describe each person. More is fine, but two or three is all you need.

When I thought of my friend, Gurdon, it was hard for me to describe him at first. He is intelligent, and he's a hard-working family guy. He's also one of the most energetic people I know – to the point of being a little too hyper sometimes. However, I admire his energy and enthusiasm for life, especially compared to my relatively low-key demeanor.

But the main thing about Gurdon is that whenever I spend time with him, I laugh. A lot. I always have a good time with him. And that ended up being the main thing I wanted to tell him.

TIP: As you are thinking about words that describe this person, you may also recall some specific memories and good times with that person. Make a note whenever you remember something specific. That may help you in Step Three.

STEP #3: RECALL YOUR FAVORITE MEMORIES

You have thought of someone you like or admire, and you have described that person. Now I want you to recall your favorite memories of that person. Think of the good times you have had together or the nice things they have done for you. Maybe there was a special experience just the two of you shared. Or maybe there was a difficult time in your life, and that person just happened to be there. (As an aside, they probably didn't *just happen* to be there; they were probably there because they knew – intuitively or otherwise – that you needed someone to lend a hand.)

Maybe it was a small thing that they did. Maybe it was something big. Maybe it was as simple as the time they said "hello" and cheered you up on a day when you were feeling down. Maybe it's something they do routinely or even every day – so much so that they may not realize how special and important they are.

Whatever it is, write it down. Also note how those experiences made you feel. Did they cheer you up when you were sad? Make you feel special when you were questioning your worth? Make you feel capable when you doubted your ability? Make you feel loved and appreciated when you were feeling alone and taken for granted?

When I thought of Miss Litoni, I recalled that she used to stop me on my way out after dinner and ask me to sit with her and say a prayer. I didn't really want to; I was ten years old and was anxious to go play with my friends. But Miss Litoni told me how much she would appreciate it – plus I knew she kept a big bowl of candy on hand for young visitors. I realize now that she was giving me the gift of her time and trying to help my mother look out for me. She made me feel that someone cared.

After you have recalled some of your favorite memories of one or more of the people on your list, you are ready for Step Four.

STEP #4: PUT IT ALL TOGETHER

Step Four might seem a bit formulaic at first, but that is not my intention.

I just want to show you how easy it is to write a thoughtful note of

appreciation. You have already done most of the work; now all you have

to do is fill in the blanks:

Dear _____ [insert name from Step #1],

You are one of the most _____ *people I know* [insert one or more of

the words you used to describe this person in Step #2].

One of my favorite memories is of the time we _____ [insert a

memory from Step #3].

Thank you.

That's it! You did it! You are free, of course, to personalize your note –

and I hope you will. It's not hard. Don't worry about getting the words

just right. They don't have to be just right. The important thing is that

you told the person how you feel. It will mean so much to them. Here

are a few examples of notes I wrote to people on my list.

To Gurdon, my friend from college:

Dear Gurdon,

You are one of the most energetic and fun people I know. I have

lots of great memories from our long friendship, including our most

recent get-together for dinner when you were in town last week.

The main thing I think of when I think of you is that I always

laugh and have a good time when you're around. Thank you for

your friendship.

Mike

To Miss Litoni, the next door neighbor from my childhood:

Dear Miss Litoni,

I often think of the times you asked me to stop and say a prayer with you before I went out to play after dinner. I probably seemed anxious to go play with my friends, and I was! But looking back, I am glad we spent the time together. You are one of the most thoughtful and caring people I know. Thank you.

Mike

To June, one of my first clients:

Dear June,

Thank you for your business. You were one of my first clients, and for that reason alone, you hold a special place with me. But you are also one of the most enjoyable people I work with. I had a great time working with you on your company's annual report, and I admire the way you keep everybody involved and on track. It's a pleasure to work with you. Thanks!

Mike

SPECIAL EVENTS AND CIRCUMSTANCES

Special events and circumstances are opportune times to share your appreciation of other people. If it's a happy occasion – a birthday, graduation, marriage or anniversary – a note from you will make it even more memorable. And if it's a sad occasion, your words can be a source of great comfort.

When I asked you to make a list of names, I said you might think of people who have passed away. They may be gone, but it's never too late to honor their memory with a note to a surviving friend or relative.

Earlier, I mentioned my Great Aunt Nina. Aunt Nina passed away, but her son, Bob (my second cousin), survived her and lives in Atlanta now. I sent him this note:

Dear Bob,

It has been many years since Aunt Nina died, but I want to let you know that I think of your mother often. My family didn't have much money when I was a kid, and Aunt Nina used to let us stay at your orange grove in Florida for our vacation. I have many fond memories from those vacations. One time Aunt Nina helped me catch a chameleon, and I used to laugh when she talked about her plans to catch an alligator from the pond by your house. She was a special person, and I will always remember her.

Your cousin,

Mike

HANDWRITTEN VS. TYPED VS. E-MAIL/TEXT

I said earlier that some people regard as "old-fashioned" the act of showing appreciation or saying "thank you." Perhaps even more old-fashioned is the notion of handwritten thank you notes.

Whether you type a message and print it out or send it via e-mail or text it, the important thing is that you share your positive feelings and let others know they are appreciated. That said, I also want to acknowledge that there is something special about the quality of the experience and the warmth of the feelings that comes with reading a personal note written in the hand of the person who gave it to you. Almost everyone I know has a handwritten thank you note from someone among their personal mementos. Recipients will save such notes and pull them out to read them time and time again. In fact, I count the note from my sister among my most prized possessions. So whenever possible, consider sending a handwritten note. But as with many things in life, how you do things is less important than what you do. That's true of thank you notes as well. So no matter how you say "thank you," give yourself an "A" for showing appreciation, and an "A+" if you do it with a handwritten note.

Tip: A friend told me that he types his notes and letters first to help him get the words right, but then he writes out the final message by hand.

NOTES TO CLIENTS AND CUSTOMERS

If you are in business, you know that it's important to say "thank you" to your customers and clients. What you may not know is that your thank you is actually a competitive advantage. In her article "The power of saying thank you," author and businesswoman Joanna Krotz describes the simple "thank you" as "an underutilized edge in the marketplace." Citing a survey that found that nearly five out of ten people don't always say thank you, Krotz notes that "so few people express appreciation… that remembering to do so is a sales point of differentiation. It goes a long way." However, it's important to remember that a thank you is just that – a thank you. If you send a customer or client a note or a card as a thank you for their business, don't ask for anything in return. Don't ask for the sale. Don't ask for a meeting. Just thank them for being your customer.

And don't stop after you thank your customers. It's also important to show appreciation to the other people you encounter in the workplace – your employees, bosses, administrative assistants, peers, suppliers and others. Research shows that when you are appreciative, your employees will be more loyal and productive, and your suppliers will go out of their way to provide good service. A note is a great way to say "thanks," but so is a kind word or a pat on the back. One of my former bosses always brought a bowl of candy to staff meetings, and team members rewarded each other with a piece of candy as a way to say "thank you" for help or for a job well done. I know it sounds silly, but people felt really good on the days they walked out of those meetings with a handful of penny candy! It doesn't take much – again, the important thing is to let people know they are appreciated.

A FINAL NOTE

I prize the note from my sister for many reasons. For one, it made me feel appreciated, which is a great gift to receive. And given our family history, Sharon's note also helped to heal years of doubt. In fact, when I wrote the story of the note and shared it with Sharon, I received another gift. When she read the passage that said, "I could never make up for the past," it made her sad – not for herself, but for me. She turned to me and said, "You don't have to make up for the past." And with those words, another weight was lifted from my life.

The note from Sharon had a profound effect on me in another way, too. It made me more appreciative in my life. Prior to that point, I did not express appreciation very often. But I came to realize that "appreciate" is a verb, and I began to pay more attention to the world around me.

I am fortunate to be surrounded by loved ones, family, friends, coworkers and others who are wonderful, generous and caring people. I have much to appreciate, and I have resolved to do a better job of showing my appreciation. I can still do better, but many people have noticed the difference. I wasn't unappreciative before. I just became more appreciative. And believe me, being more appreciative will have a positive effect on your life and on the lives of the people you touch.

I want to leave you with a final thought. What if you wrote 52 thank you notes over the next 52 weeks? Most people laugh when I suggest writing 52 notes. But that's just one short thank you note per week. Think about all the good feelings you would create if you wrote one note per week – and think about how those good feelings would be multiplied if each recipient wrote a note, and so on, and so on. The world would truly be a better place, and much of it would be *thanks to you*.

Mike O'Mary is Founding Dreamer at dreamofthings.com

At times, our own light goes out and is rekindled

by a spark from another person. Each of us has cause to think

with deep gratitude of those who have lighted

the flame within us. Albert Schweitzer

Gratitude is the memory of the heart. Italian proverb

For more information, including helpful advice, gift books, greeting cards, free e-cards, and videos that you can share with family and friends, please visit:

dreamofthings.com